About This Book

Title: *Sand Dunes*

Step: 4

Word Count: 179

Skills in Focus: Silent e

Tricky Words: deserts, into, over, blows, some, cover, few, grow, beach, sea

Ideas for Using This Book

Before Reading:

- **Comprehension:** Look at the title and cover image together. Walk through the pictures in the book with readers and have them make predictions about what they might learn while reading. Help them make connections by asking what they already know about sand dunes.
- **Accuracy:** Practice saying the tricky words listed on page 1.
- **Phonics:** Write the word *dome* on a piece of paper. Point to the pattern *o_e* in the word. Explain that the silent *e* makes the vowel before it have a long sound, saying its own name. Model how to say each sound in the word *dome* slowly in isolation. Then blend the sounds together smoothly to say the whole word. Explain that in some words, such as *dunes*, the vowel *u* doesn't quite say its own name. It makes the /oo/ sound. Offer additional silent *e* examples from the book, such as *time*, *snake*, and *slope*.

During Reading:

- Have readers point under each word as they read it.
- **Decoding:** If readers are stuck on a word, help them say each sound and blend the sounds together smoothly. You may want to point out words with silent *e* as they appear.
- **Comprehension:** Invite students to talk about what new things they are learning about sand dunes while reading. What are they learning that they didn't know before?

After Reading:

Discuss the book. Some ideas for questions:

- What are some places where you might see sand dunes?
- What do you still wonder about sand dunes?

Sand Dunes

Text by Laura Stickney

Reading Consultant
Deborah MacPhee, PhD
Professor, School of Teaching and Learning
Illinois State University

PICTURE WINDOW BOOKS
a capstone imprint

Sand dunes are hills and slopes of sand.

The wind shapes the sand into dunes.

Sand dunes change shape over time.

The wind blows and shifts the dunes.

Some sand dunes are big.

They cover
wide spaces.
They make
huge domes.

In some places, you can sled and slide on the slopes of dunes.

Sand dunes
can be small.

Dunes can be flat or bumpy.

Sand dunes have 2 sides.

The wind hits one side of the dune.

The dune's other side is the slip face. No wind hits it.

wind
slip face

Deserts can have lots of big sand dunes.

These places can get hot when the sun shines. There is no shade.

Sand dunes have few plants.

But a bush or shrub can grow on a dune's slope.

Bugs and rats live on sand dunes.

They hide in the hills.

Snakes slip and slide on the sandy slopes.

A beach can
have sand dunes.

The dunes take shape at the edge of the sea.

The wind and waves make sand into domes.

You can race and dance on sand dunes!

More Ideas:

Phonemic Awareness Activity

Writing with Silent *e*:
Challenge students to write a short story about sand dunes using as many silent *e* words as they can think of. The story can be as serious or as silly as they'd like!

Suggested words:

- dune
- shape
- domes
- snakes
- huge
- slide
- slope
- race
- face
- wide
- hide

Extended Learning Activity

Drawing a Desert:
Show readers a few photographs of sandy deserts around the world. Then ask readers to draw a picture of a desert. Have them write about the landscapes in their drawings. What plants grow there? What kinds of animals live there? Challenge readers to use words with silent *e* in their descriptions.

Published by Picture Window Books, an imprint of Capstone
1710 Roe Crest Drive, North Mankato, Minnesota 56003
capstonepub.com

Library of Congress Cataloging-in-Publication Data is available on the Library of Congress website.

ISBN: 9798875277627 (hardback)
ISBN: 9798875277580 (paperback)
ISBN: 9798875277566 (eBook PDF)

Image Credits: Getty: DEBOVE SOPHIE, 30, Giselleflissak, 1, 13, Gunter Nuyts, 7, hadynyah, 18, 32, LucVi, front cover, rusm, 28–29, SHansche, 4–5; Shutterstock: Arodel, 12, Chanitada, 27, EvaL Miko, 19, Gambarini Gianandrea, 8–9, iamlukyeee, 26, NileshShah, 24–25, oliveromg, 20–21, Ondrej Prosicky, 22–23, PSD photography, 10–11, back cover, QQQQQQQT, 2–3, Repina Valeriya, 6, Yerbolat Shadrakhov, 14–15, zombiu26, 16–17

Printed and bound in China. PO 6460